We're Going on a *Bear Hunt*

My Adventure Field Guide

WALKER
ENTERTAINMENT

– Contents –

Nature, Nature Everywhere!

Come rain or shine, the world is a beautiful place. From creepy-crawlies in your home, towering trees in the forest or the sound of mud squelching under your boots – nature is everywhere!

Whether you want to observe the plants in your house or step outside to explore, you can use this Field Guide to learn about the things you might see on your journey.

Plan your adventure

Before you start your adventure, you'll need to think about what to take with you and how to stay safe along the way. Here is a list of things you might want to pack in your rucksack.

If it's hot, then make sure you have:
- suncream
- a hat
- water

If it's cold, then wrap up with:
- a hat
- a scarf
- mittens
- warm socks

If it's raining, don't forget:
- wellies
- waterproofs
- an umbrella

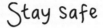

Stay safe

While exploring nature is great fun, it is important to do it safely. Here are some simple dos and don'ts to keep you out of harm's way:

- Never travel alone – always explore with a responsible adult.
- Take care when crossing roads.
- Don't touch or eat any plants unless you know it is safe to do so.
- Don't touch creatures unless you know it is safe to do so – and always treat them kindly.
- Keep an eye on the time to avoid being out after dark.
- Pack some plasters and antiseptic cream.
- Wear comfortable boots or shoes.
- If you're going really far, take some food and water for your journey.

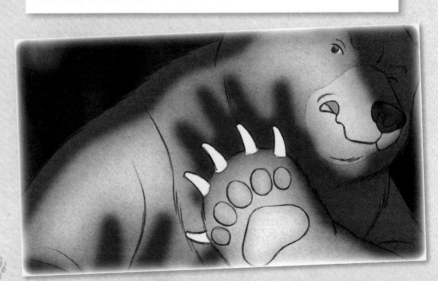

There's a whole world out there

Whether you live in the country or in the city, have your own back garden or play in the park – there are all sorts of places that you can explore.

At home

Gaze at the night sky through the windows, study any pets carefully and hunt for house spiders if you dare!

At school

Mind your step – look for plants growing in the cracks of the playground. Can you see birds nesting in the roof?

FIELD ACTIVITY

Why not ask your teacher if you can make a vegetable patch at school?

In the countryside

Feel the mud, grass and leaves under your boots and see how many animals you can spot along the way.

At the seaside

The water's edge is bustling with life – it's fantastic fun to see what lurks in the rock pools.

Take note

Why not keep a nature journal? It's a nice way to keep a record of the things you see. Plus, it's fun to observe, write and draw.

There is no right or wrong way to keep a nature journal. All you need is:

- a notebook
- a pen or pencil
- tape or glue
- small bags for collecting nature treasure
- lots of enthusiasm!

Are you ready to **run** through the grass,

splash through water and

squelch through mud?

If so, then **jump right in!**

13

High in the Sky

The big, blue sky

When you start your adventure, look up at the sky. It can look very different from day to day and the colour of the sky can really create a sense of mood.

IMPORTANT NOTE

Make sure that you never look directly into the sun, as it can harm your eyes.

Why is the sky blue?

Light is made up of a stream of colours. As light waves move through the **atmosphere**, they bump into particles of dust or water droplets. When light hits these particles it scatters in different directions. Blue light is scattered more effectively than other colours – and this is why the sky normally appears blue.

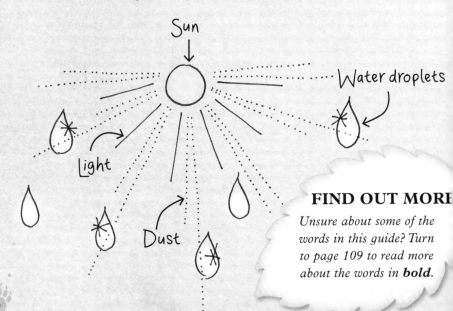

Sun

Water droplets

Light

Dust

FIND OUT MORE

*Unsure about some of the words in this guide? Turn to page 109 to read more about the words in **bold**.*

Why does the sky sometimes look red?

At sunrise or sunset the sun is lower on the horizon.
The sun's light waves have to travel further to get to
our eyes and so only the red light makes it through.

"Red sky at night,
shepherds' delight.
Red sky in the morning,
shepherds' warning."

Long ago, this rhyme was used to forecast the weather.
If the morning sky is red, then rain clouds are likely
to come in from the west. But if the evening sky is red,
then the sky will probably be clear.

See the light

The light that we see travels as a wave and each colour has a **wavelength**. You can use a prism or a glass of water to break light into its rainbow-coloured parts. These are the colours of the light **spectrum** – the same ones that we can see in a rainbow.

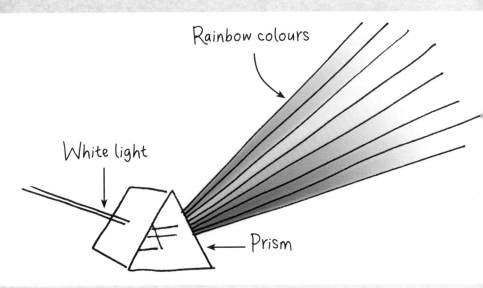

Rainbow colours

White light

Prism

What is a rainbow?

You might see a rainbow if the sun is low in the sky behind you and there is rain in front of you. When the sun's light hits the raindrops, the light bends – this causes each colour to leave the raindrops at its own angle, making a colourful arc in the sky.

Red   Orange   Yellow   Green   Blue   Indigo   Violet

Wonderful weather

We all know about the weather – it's all people seem to talk about! But do you *really* know about the weather and why it changes from one day to the next?

Why does it rain?

When a lot of water droplets gather in the clouds, the clouds become heavy. **Gravity** then causes the water droplets to fall as rain.

FIND OUT MORE

See pages 38–39 to learn more about rain.

Why does the wind blow?

It's all to do with the weight of air. When the sun shines, the air near the ground gets warmer. Warm air rises and cooler air moves under it. This moving air is wind.

What are clouds?

When warm air rises from the ground, it takes **water vapour** with it. This air cools as it gets higher in the sky, causing the vapour to turn into liquid and attach itself to floating dust particles. These water droplets join together to make clouds.

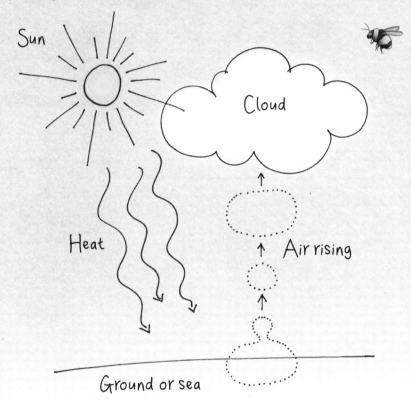

Sun

Cloud

Heat

Air rising

Ground or sea

FIELD FACT

As a cloud gathers more water droplets, it gets thicker and less light travels through it. This is why rain clouds make the sky look grey.

Name that cloud

Clouds are put into groups based on their shape and how high they are in the sky. Here are some of the most common groups:

Cirrus

Thin and wispy clouds that form high in the sky.

Stratus

A low-level layer of clouds that blanket the sky.

Nimbostratus

A low level of dark grey rain or snow clouds.

Cumulonimbus

Thunderclouds that cause heavy rain.

Cumulus

White puffy clouds that look like cotton wool.

What are snowflakes?

Snowflakes are ice **crystals**. They form in clouds when the temperature is below freezing.

What is lightning?

Lightning is a bright flash of electricity produced by a thunderstorm. When the icy raindrops in a thundercloud collide, electrical charges are created. When the positive and negative charges grow large enough, electricity jumps between them and this is lightning.

The night sky

As day turns into night and it gets colder, there is still plenty going on in the sky. The moon travels around the earth in a circle called an **orbit** and appears to change shape each night. These different shapes are called "phases of the moon". You will see them over the course of a month.

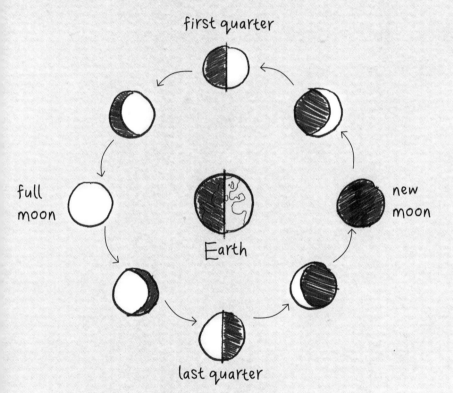

first quarter

full moon

Earth

new moon

last quarter

Why does the moon change shape?

The moon is always round but at certain points in its journey, it catches more of the sun's light than at others. The parts that are lit up are what we see, and this is why the moon *appears* to change shape.

Around the world

Have you wondered why you only ever see one side of the moon? Try facing an object (imagining that it is earth). Move around the object showing your face to it the whole time. Notice how you rotate once around the object without ever showing it your back?

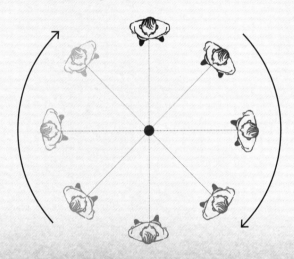

What is an eclipse?

When the earth passes between the sun and the moon, it casts a shadow on the moon. This is called a lunar eclipse.

When the moon passes between the earth and the sun, it casts a shadow on the earth. This is called a solar eclipse.

IMPORTANT NOTE

Do not look directly at a solar eclipse unless you have special eclipse glasses.

What are tides?

The moon's **gravity** causes the oceans to bulge out in the direction of the moon. This movement of the rising and falling sea is called a tide. When the gravitational pull is at its highest point, the result is a high tide. When the pull is at its lowest point, we see a low tide.

What are stars?

Stars are huge balls of glowing gas. They form when **gravity** pulls enough dust and gas together. The mass gets hotter and hotter, until powerful reactions occur and a young star is made. Even the sun is a star!

It really is a bear hunt!

There are billions of stars in the universe. Ancient Greek stargazers often named star patterns (**constellations**) after animals from their stories or myths.

The Ursa Major **constellation** is known as the "Great Bear", and its seven brightest stars (in yellow) make up the Plough.

The Ursa Minor is sometimes called the "Little Bear". The Polaris star is the brightest star in the Little Bear **constellation**. It is also known as the North Star as it points to the north.

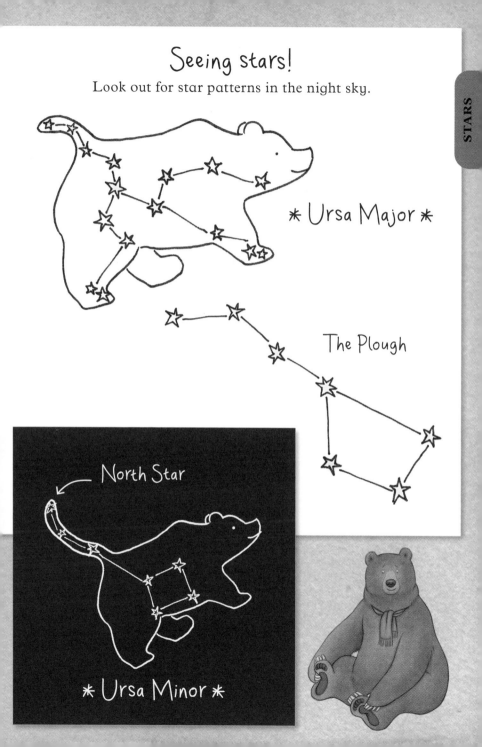

Seeing stars!

Look out for star patterns in the night sky.

* Ursa Major *

The Plough

North Star

* Ursa Minor *

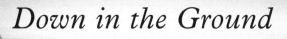

Down in the Ground

What's under your feet?

Have you ever wondered about what's beneath you? There are many useful natural materials hidden away below the earth's surface ... dig deeper to find out more!

Soil

Soil covers much of the earth's land. It is made up of air, water, minerals and **organic material** (dead plants and animals).

Minerals

A mineral is a solid, natural non-living substance, such as clay, salt or sand.

Clay

Clay is made up of tiny particles of rock carried from one place to another by water. When wet, it can be easily moulded into different shapes.

Silt

Silt is created when rock is worn away by water and ice. It is made up of particles that are larger than clay but smaller than sand.

x

Sand

Sand is simply small, loose grains of disintegrated rock.

Bacteria

Bacteria break down dead plants and animals and recycle **nutrients** in the soil. A teaspoon of soil can contain up to one billion **bacteria**!

FIELD FACT

The largest living thing on earth is a honey fungus! It measures 3.8 kilometres across and can be found in the Blue Mountains in Oregon, USA.

Fungus

Fungi have a "fruit" part that grows out of the ground as a mushroom. The rest of a fungus lives in the soil and is made up of thread-like strands that spread throughout the ground.

IMPORTANT NOTE

Mushrooms can be poisonous. Never eat them unless you know they are safe.

Thick oozy mud

Mud is just soil mixed with water. It might be mucky, but it has its uses...

Happy as a pig in mud

Pigs roll in mud to keep cool. The dried mud acts like suncream and also protects the pigs from biting insects.

Worms

Earthworms are a gardener's best friend. They eat their own weight in soil and **organic material** each day and then poo out piles (or "casts"), making nourishing compost as they go.

Mud bricks

Mud bricks are made from mud that is baked in the sun. They were one of the first building materials to be used in ancient times and many countries still use them today.

Make your own mud bricks

You will need:

Ice cream tubs
A bucket
A large mixing spoon
Soil and water

1. Collect a few old containers, such as ice cream tubs.

2. Put some soil and water into a bucket, then mix using a spoon.

3. Fill each of your containers with the mud. You can try adding different things – such as grass, sand or straw – to each mixture to see how they turn out.

4. Leave your bricks to bake in the sun for a couple of days, then carefully remove them by overturning the containers.

It's about to get rocky

Rocks are made up of many tiny pieces that can be different colours, shapes and sizes. There are three main groups of rocks:

Igneous

Igneous rocks are made up of **crystals** that form when red-hot liquid (magma) erupts from volcanoes and then cools. If the magma cools slowly, large **crystals** form. If it cools quickly then small **crystals** form. Granite is an example of an igneous rock.

Sedimentary

Sedimentary rocks are made up of rock particles and dead sea creatures that are carried by water or wind to lakes and oceans. The layers settle and are compressed over millions of years. Examples include chalk and limestone.

Metamorphic

Metamorphic rocks are made when extreme heat or pressure causes one type of rock to change into another. They are usually unaffected by weather and are very hard-wearing. Slate and marble are examples of metamorphic rock.

FIELD ACTIVITY

Why not start your own rock collection? Can you get an example of the three types?

Fossils

Fossils are an excellent way for us to learn about animals and plants that lived millions of years ago. There are two main types of fossil: body fossils (of an animal or plant) and trace fossils (such as footprints and nests).

Fossils can be formed when hard body parts, such as bones, are covered by layers of mud or sand. Over time the parts are gradually replaced by minerals. Impressions, such as footprints, can be covered by layers of mud or sand, which eventually become rock.

FIELD FACT

Sometimes animals and plants were preserved in amber (a hardened tree sap).

FIELD FACT

Did you know that poo can be fossilized? This is called a coprolite.

Moving mountains

What we call a hill and what we call a mountain has not been agreed on around the world. However, mountains are generally higher and steeper than hills. There are five main types of mountain:

Fold (or folded)

Fold mountains are the most common type of mountain. They form when pieces of the earth's crust – called **tectonic plates** – collide and their edges crumple up.

Fold it up

Try pushing a piece of paper together to see how it folds.

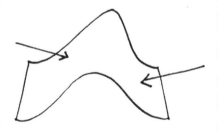

Fault-Block (or block)

Fault-block mountains form when cracks (or faults) in the earth's crust force some blocks of rock up and others down. This often creates mountains with a long slope on one side and a sharp drop on the other.

Dome

Dome mountains form when liquid magma pushes up from under the earth's crust. The magma does not break through, but makes the land blow up like a balloon.

Volcanic

Volcanic mountains form when volcanoes erupt and mounds of ash and lava eventually cool and harden into rock. Rock and lava pile up, layer upon layer. Over time, a mountain forms.

Plateau

Plateaus are large, flat areas of high ground that form when colliding **tectonic plates** push up the land without folding. They are shaped by rivers and streams, which leave deep valleys next to high cliffs.

FIELD FACT

The Himalayas mountain range in South Asia is made up of fold mountains. Nine of the highest peaks on the planet stand here, including Mount Everest at about 8,850 metres above sea level.

The water cycle

Water is the lifeline to every living thing on the planet. It can be found in the ground, in the air and even inside your body! Water moves all around the earth in a constant cycle – between the sea, air and land.

1. The heat of the sun causes water from rivers, lakes or the sea to **evaporate** (change from liquid into vapour like the steam from a kettle). The steam rises up into the **atmosphere**.

2. Trees and plants also release **water vapour** through pores in their leaves – a process known as **transpiration**.

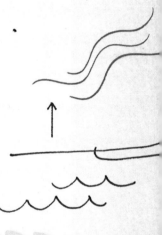

FIND OUT MORE

Flick to page 67 to find out more about leaves.

FIELD ACTIVITY

Why not collect rainwater to water the plants in your garden?

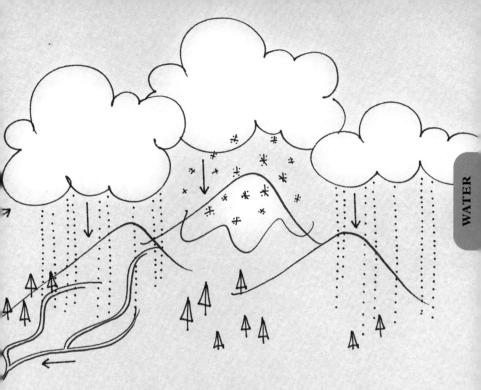

3. **Water vapour** in the air gets cold and changes back into liquid, forming clouds – a process called **condensation**.

4. When the clouds get full of water, they become heavy and water drops in the form of rain or snow. This is called **precipitation**.

5. When the rain or snow falls, it may soak back into the earth and become part of the groundwater that plants and animals drink; or it may collect in rivers, lakes or oceans – and the whole cycle starts again.

A vanishing act

Some materials **dissolve** (become absorbed into liquid) when they are added to water. Put a teaspoon of each of these materials into a glass of water and stir. Can you record which ones **dissolve**?

Salt

Sand

Jelly

Why is the sea salty?

Some of the salt in the sea comes from volcanic vents or rocks on the seabed, but most comes from land. When it rains, mineral salts are washed from the ground into rivers, which flow to the sea.

FIELD FACT

About ninety-seven per cent of all earth's water is held in the salty sea. That means about three per cent is fresh water.

Fussy fish?

Some fish can only live in salt water, while some can only live in fresh water. A saltwater fish drinks seawater but excretes salt.

A freshwater fish will drink fresh water but excrete excess water. Some fish, like salmon, undergo changes which allow them to travel between fresh and salt water.

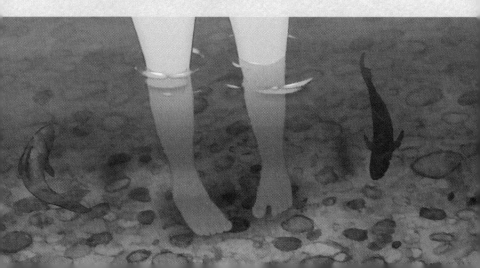

Further Afield

Urban nature

Nature is everywhere, but sometimes we forget to notice. You may live in a town or city, but there are still plenty of natural wonders to be found right under your nose.

FIELD ACTIVITY

What is it like where you live? What can you see, touch, hear and smell?

Spiders

Cobwebs might look spooky, but did you know that they are made from silk? This silk is five times stronger than a strand of steel of the same size.

Dogs and cats

Dogs and cats are common household pets, but dogs share an ancestor with wolves. Cats share an ancestor with lions.

Birds and wasps

Birds and wasps make nests in chimneys. Some birds also like to nest under eaves (where the roof overhangs the building) and even under bridges.

Rats and mice

Rats feel at home in a town or city, hiding out in sewers or tunnels. Mice are agile creatures – capable of swimming, climbing and even jumping!

FIELD ACTIVITY

Why not keep a list of all the animals you have spotted near your house?

In the country

You might live near to fields and hills as far as the eye can see. Or maybe you've just taken a day trip. Either way, there's plenty to see out in the country!

Hedgerows

These "bushy" fences are home to a wide range of wildlife including butterflies, birds and mice. Sadly many hedgerows are being lost.

Orchards

In spring, fruit trees are covered in beautiful **blossoms**. Tucked inside the bottom of each **blossom** are the seeds that will eventually turn into fruit.

FIND OUT MORE

Turn to page 62 to read more about flowering plants.

Fields

Farmers play an important part in producing all of our food and tend to their fields of crops daily.

Hills

Hills are easier to climb than mountains and should give you an amazing view. While some are created naturally (in similar ways to mountains), others are man-made.

FIELD ACTIVITY

Hills may once have been built as a place to stare at the stars. Why not gaze at the stars from the top of a hill?

Yummy baked apples

If you visit an orchard in autumn, you'll be able to pick apples. You could also take blackberries from hedgerows (but leave some for the birds). Here's a delicious way to enjoy your picked fruit.

Ingredients:

6 apples, washed
100g blackberries, washed
30g butter
2 tsp brown sugar
40g raisins
ice cream

1. Ask an adult to preheat the oven to 150°C / gas mark 2.

2. Have an adult help you to core the apples.

3. Mix together the butter, sugar and raisins in a bowl.

4. Half fill each apple with the mixture, then add a couple of blackberries on top.

5. Bake the stuffed apples for about 20–30 minutes until soft.

6. Serve warm with ice cream.

* Always ask for adult supervision and follow the recipe carefully.

Woodland walks

Do you have a wood or forest near you? Then pull on your wellies and go on a family trek – you can even take your friends.

There is life going on at all levels of the wood, whether up in the trees or down in the **burrows**...

FIELD ACTIVITY

Stand in the woods and close your eyes. How many sounds can you hear?

On the Ground

The woodland floor is crawling with wildlife. Layers of fallen leaves called "leaf litter" are home to slugs, snails, worms, spiders, beetles, millipedes and centipedes.

Leaf litter contains millions of **bacteria** and **fungi,** which break the litter down into **nutrients** that a tree can absorb.

FIELD ACTIVITY

Have a look under leaves on the woodland floor and see what you can find in the leaf litter.

Life on the river

Rivers are everywhere – in towns and cities as well as the countryside. The place where a river starts is called the **source** and the place where it meets the sea is called the **mouth**.

Many rivers and streams join together before they reach the sea. The smaller ones are called **tributaries**. On a steep slope, a river flows fast. When the ground flattens out, the river will start to curve and bend.

A river food chain

Food chains show us how each living thing gets food and how **nutrients** and energy are passed from creature to creature. Here's one example of a river food chain:

FIELD ACTIVITY

What did you have for dinner last night? Can you draw the food chain in a journal?

Sun

Plankton

Crustacean

Fish

RIVER

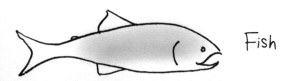

River residents

Look out for some of the following wildlife living on the river.

Snails

All snails belong to a group called **molluscs** – animals with a soft unsegmented body and no backbone. Some species of snail live in fresh water.

Swans

The swan is the largest member of the duck and goose family. Those from the northern parts of the world usually have white feathers. Those from the south tend to be almost black with white wing feathers that can be seen when they fly.

Otters

If you're very lucky, you might spot an otter! Otters are excellent swimmers because of their streamlined bodies – and can stay underwater for up to eight minutes.

Dragonflies

The dragonfly darts about near fresh water eating other flying insects. The young larvae, called nymphs (which live in the water), can take up to a year to become winged adults.

From egg to frog

Some creatures prefer life in the slow lane – like frogs, which lay their frogspawn (eggs) in slow-moving streams or ponds. Frogs are **amphibians**, meaning they live on land and in water. Frogs go through several different stages before becoming an adult. This is called **metamorphosis.**

Between 700 and 2,000 eggs are laid at a time.

Up to 16 weeks after hatching, the froglets become adult frogs.

The eggs hatch into tiny tadpoles after 1 week.

7 weeks after hatching, the tadpoles grow back legs.

12 weeks after hatching, the tadpoles turn into froglets with stumpy tails.

Curious caves

If you follow a river far enough, you will reach the seaside and may even find a cave! Caves are mysterious places – but do you know how they got there?

Caves start life as a part of the cliff face, which is constantly pounded by the sea. The softer parts of rock **erode** much more quickly than the rest of it. Eventually a hollow is cut out, which widens and deepens to become a cave.

Inside some caves are pointy bits of rock called **stalactites** and **stalagmites**. Stalactites hang down from the ceiling. Stalagmites point up from the ground.

Stalactites

When water flows down through the ground and into a cave, it **dissolves** a mineral called **calcite** and carries it through cracks in the ceiling. The **calcite** slowly builds up into a **stalactite**, which hangs down like an icicle.

Stalagmites

Water from the end of the **stalactite** leaves more **calcite** in a pile on the cave floor, and a **stalagmite** forms. That's why stalactites and stalagmites are usually found in pairs.

FIELD FACT

Sometimes bears will sleep in caves in colder parts of the world, but they will not live there permanently.

Tiny Plants and Tall Trees

Plenty of plants

There are so many kinds of plant, including grasses, ferns, mosses, flowers and trees. As well as providing essential oxygen, plants also form the base of most food chains – without them nothing could survive.

What is a plant?

A plant is an **organism** made up of many cells. Plants can make their own food (**glucose**) by a process called **photosynthesis**. This happens when the leaves on a plant absorb light and the energy changes **carbon dioxide** and water into a sugar called **glucose**. Oxygen is produced as a by-product.

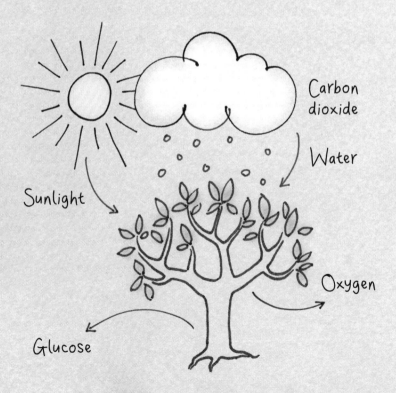

Carbon dioxide

Water

Sunlight

Oxygen

Glucose

Where do plants live?

Plants can live on land, in the water and on other plants.

Epiphytes

Epiphytes grow harmlessly upon other plants (such as trees) and get their moisture and **nutrients** from the air and rain. Mosses and orchids are both good examples of epiphytes.

Parasites

Parasitic plants live on other plants (or hosts). They take all the **nutrients** and water from their hosts, sometimes damaging their hosts in the process.

Choosy plants

Some plants like sunny, high and dry places. Others prefer shady, low and wet areas. A plant that usually lives under a canopy of tall trees is likely to prefer a shady **environment**, as it has developed broader, thinner leaves to absorb as much light as possible. If the plant was put into direct sunlight, it may absorb too much sun and die.

FIELD FACT

*Plants can warn each other of pests using their roots and thread-like strands from **fungi**. They then release chemicals to scare pests away.*

Homegrown habitats

It's easy to grow your own plants at home. Why not give it a try and record your observations as the plant grows?

You will need:

Sprouting seeds (such as cress)
3 small containers
Cotton wool
Water
A plastic bag or cling film

1. Put a piece of damp cotton wool in the bottom of each container. Sprinkle the seeds onto the cotton wool and press the seeds down gently.

2. Ask an adult to help you cover the pots with cling film or a plastic bag and put in a warm place (a windowsill is ideal).

3. Check every day and make sure the cotton wool does not dry out (add a little water if you think it is getting dry).

4. Once you can see small shoots, remove the cling film or plastic bag and leave the containers in a warm and sunny place for a week.

5. Keep checking to make sure the cotton wool does not dry out and take note as your plant grows.

FIELD ACTIVITY

Once the seeds have sprouted, ask an adult to help you plant them.

Picking flowers

Flowers are very pretty and can smell nice, but that's not just for our benefit! They put on a show to attract **pollinators**, which carry their pollen to other flowers in a process called pollination. Flowers come in many colours, shapes and sizes but most have a similar structure.

Petals

Many flowers have colourful petals to attract insects and animals.

Stamen

Stamens produce dust-like grains, called pollen.

Carpel

The stigma, style and ovary make up the carpel. The stigma receives the pollen from a **pollinator**. The pollen travels through the style to the ovary, which produces more seeds.

Sepal

Sepals are leaf-like outer parts of the flower that protect the bud until it opens.

Nectary

Nectaries are glands that ooze out a sugary fluid to attract **pollinators**.

FIELD ACTIVITY

Can you pick apart a flower to see if you can find the parts listed here?

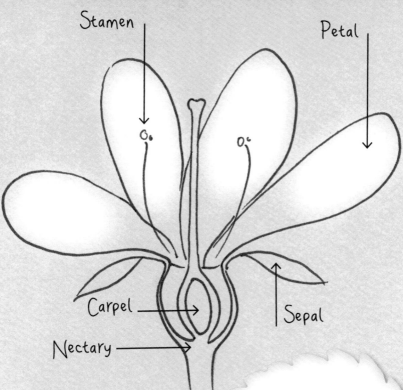

Stamen

Petal

Carpel

Nectary

Sepal

FIELD FACT

You might not think it, but trees, grasses and even cacti produce flowers!

Pollinators

Plants have helpers who move the pollen for them so that they can make seeds and reproduce. Just like plants, these **pollinators** come in all shapes and sizes. They can be insects (bees and butterflies), animals (such as birds and bats) and even humans.

Here is an example of how it all happens:

1. A bee drinks a flower's nectar and pollen sticks to its body.

2. The bee visits a second flower and transfers the pollen to this flower's stigma.

3. The pollen travels down the style to the ovary. This fertilises the egg cells, which turn into seeds.

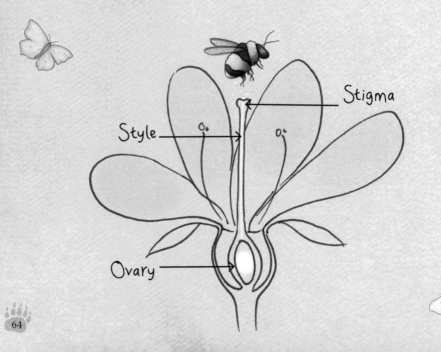

Stigma

Style

Ovary

Seed journey

In order for new plants to grow from the seeds, the seeds must leave the plant. This happens in many ways:

Fruit

Many plants produce tasty fruit which animals eat. The seeds then come out in the animals' poo!

Wind

Some plants have seeds that are specially designed to travel in the wind.

Animals

Some seeds are covered in hooks or sticky mucus and hitch a ride on the fur of passing animals before falling off.

Humans

Humans can help by planting seeds – either by buying them from shops or collecting them from the wild.

Bursting seeds

Some plants do their own work when dispersing seeds. The fruits dry up and create seed heads, which burst open, forcing the seeds out.

Tall, tall trees

Trees are the biggest plants on the planet. They cover large areas of land and are home to many living things – even other plants. Trees are important as they provide us with oxygen that we need to breathe. There are two main types of tree:

Deciduous trees

Deciduous trees are huge flowering plants. Most **deciduous** trees are broadleaved, and every autumn these trees shed their leaves to save energy.

Evergreens

Evergreens look green throughout the year. Although they do lose leaves, most lose them gradually. When people think of **evergreen** trees they often think of conifers (such as Christmas trees). They have thin or needle-like leaves and their seeds come from cones instead of flowers.

Leaf shapes

There are many technical names used for leaf shapes but here are just a few that describe the edges (or **margins**):

Sage leaf
entire shaped

Beech leaf
serrated shaped

Oak leaf
lobed shaped

FIELD ACTIVITY

Have you seen any colourful leaves? Why not collect some and stick them in a journal?

The veins of a leaf support the plant and transport the water and **nutrients** that it needs. Leaves also help to identify plants. The surface of a leaf is covered in tiny pores called **stomata**.

The **stomata** open to allow plants to "breathe" in **carbon dioxide** for **photosynthesis**. As the stomata open, **water vapour** is also lost in a process called **transpiration**. This lost moisture is replaced by water sucked up through a plant's roots.

Tree houses

It's not just humans that need trees. Trees provide many creatures with homes, food and shelter.

Birds

Birds use twigs and leaves to make their nests in the safety of the branches.

Insects

Insects such as caterpillars and beetles feed on the leaves. Some beetles may tunnel into the bark and lay their eggs.

Squirrels

Squirrels forage for nuts on the forest floor, storing them to survive over winter.

Other Plants

Other tiny plants can grow on the tree bark, such as **algae**, **lichen** and moss.

FIELD FACT

Lichen can be found in a variety of colours and is a sign of good air quality.

How tall is tall?

Trees are some of the oldest and tallest plants on the planet – but how can you tell just how tall they are? Ask an adult to help you with this simple exercise to estimate the height of a tree.

Pick a tree to guess the height of. Ask an adult to stand near to the tree.

Stand back from the tree and guess how many times the height of your adult goes into the height of the tree.

Write down your guess.

Next, using a metre ruler measure the height of your adult (in centimetres).

Write down the height.

Times the two measurements together. This number roughly equals the height of the tree.

Incredible Creepy-Crawlies

Bugs everywhere!

You must have seen them – there are millions of bugs creeping and crawling all over the world! The word "bug" is often used to describe all insects but a true bug is a particular kind of insect. Do you know what a true insect is?

What is an insect?

Insects belong to a large group of creatures called **arthropods**, which means "jointed legs". This group includes many creatures that are not insects, such as spiders, woodlice, millipedes and centipedes.

All **arthropods** have jointed legs and a hard outer skeleton, but no backbone. However, an insect has three segmented body parts (the head, thorax and abdomen), plus six legs.

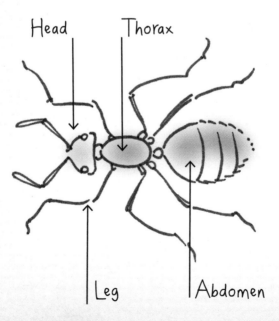

Head   Thorax

Leg   Abdomen

True bugs

"True bugs" don't bite into their food. Instead, they inject juices into prey with their beak-like mouths and then suck it up. Most true bugs have two pairs of wings.

Beetles

If you see a creature with a hard wing case, it is likely to be a beetle. The beetle's hard front wings fold over the soft hind wings, when not in use, like a protective shield.

The search for bugs!

When you next go outside, lift up a rock and see what's hiding there. Can you:

Count the legs on any insects that you find?

See if any of the creatures have hard wing cases?

Spot any true bugs?

Flying high

There are many other winged insects. Flying skills help them to survive. They can quickly escape from hunters, and go long distances to find mates and food.

Dragonflies and damselflies

You can tell the difference between a dragonfly and a damselfly by watching them at rest. Dragonflies hold their wings out wide like an aeroplane, while damselflies close up their wings.

Flies

With no jaws, flies can only eat liquid food. They turn solid food into liquid by vomiting onto it before sucking it up!

Butterflies and moths

These delicate insects flitter and flutter around our heads, showing off their beautiful wing patterns. Butterflies tend to come out at daytime to warm their flight muscles in the sun. Most moths come out at night and warm up by vibrating their wings.

Butterflies and moths start out as caterpillars, which hatch from eggs. They eat and grow, then form a **chrysalis**. The caterpillar undergoes an amazing transformation inside, finally emerging as a moth or butterfly!

egg   caterpillar   chrysalis   butterfly

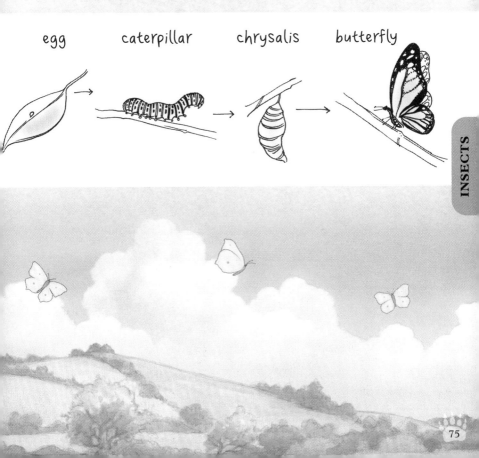

Living together

Some insects live and work together in groups called **colonies**. Numbers in the groups can range from thousands to millions! Each member of the group has a job to do, from finding food to looking after the nest.

FIELD ACTIVITY

Can you spot any insect colonies in the garden or further afield?

Ants

Believe it or not, ants are actually related to wasps and bees. Ants evolved from wasp-like ancestors millions of years ago.

Bees and wasps

Wasps are more brightly coloured than bees, and bees are rounder and hairier. Bees feed on nectar and pollen, while wasps eat fruit, nectar and other insects.

Grasshoppers

These cleverly coloured creatures are well **camouflaged** (hidden) from enemies and can hop away for a quick escape.

More garden critters

Although none of the following are insects or bugs, they can still be spotted living nearby!

Spiders

Spiders are eight-legged meat-eaters. They trap insect prey in webs before injecting them with venomous fangs to stop the insects moving.

Woodlice

There are thought to be over 3,000 different species of woodlouse around the world. Some can roll themselves up into an almost perfect ball to protect themselves.

FIELD FACT

*Snails and slugs are not insects or **arthropods**. Can you remember which group the freshwater snail belongs to? That will give you a clue!*

Centipedes and millipedes

Most centipedes have thirty-five pairs of legs on average and can move quickly, while most millipedes have up to two hundred pairs of legs and move slowly.

Earthworms

These slithering creatures belong to a large group of segmented worms called **annelids**. They live in the soil and play a crucial role in breaking the soil down – allowing **bacteria** to feed on it and release the **nutrients**.

Build a worm farm

Why not make a worm farm to see these clever creatures in action? You will need:

A glass jar with lid   Soil and leaves
A sheet of black paper   Water

1. Take a jar and fill it with alternate layers of soil and sand, leaving a small gap at the top.

2. Collect some earthworms and carefully put them in the jar.

3. Add some old leaves, vegetable peelings or overripe fruit.

4. Ask an adult to make some small holes in the lid of the jar, then screw on the lid.

5. Place black paper around the jar and put it into a cool, dark cupboard.

6. Always keep your worm farm moist (but not too damp) and check there is enough food.

7. Check on it every few days to see what's happening – but remember to return the worms to their natural **habitat** when you're done!

Extraordinary Creatures

On the wing

Birds are extraordinary creatures that take to skies all over the world – tweeting, squawking and chirping as they go. Birds belong to the group of animals called **vertebrates**, meaning animals with a backbone (you are a vertebrate). All birds share the same basic features.

Light bones

Bird bones are hollow with a honeycomb-like centre. This makes birds light enough to fly.

Flight feathers

Birds have different feathers for different jobs. "Flight feathers" are found on the tail and the wings and provide "lift". Imagine your arm is a wing. Primary flight feathers line your lower arm and secondary flight feathers line your upper arm.

Downy feathers

Downy feathers are soft fluffy feathers found on a bird's body that keep the bird warm.

FIELD FACT

Did you know that birds are descended from dinosaurs?

Shaft

The shaft is the supporting part of the feather that runs through the middle.

Vane

The vane is the flat part of a feather found on both sides of the shaft.

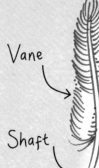

Vane

Shaft

IMPORTANT NOTE

If you see an egg or baby chick that has fallen out of the nest, do not touch it – the parents may be nearby.

Eggs

Birds lay a wonderful variety of eggs. The largest egg in the world belongs to the ostrich and is roughly the size of twenty-four hen eggs! Hummingbirds tend to have the smallest eggs, which can be less than one centimetre long.

Migration

Many birds move (**migrate**) around the world, from their breeding grounds in the north to their wintering homes in the south. Look for large flocks of birds flying in formation in spring and autumn.

A cake fit for a bird

In winter, birds may find it hard to find food. You can help by making a bird cake for them.

You will need:

Yogurt pots   String
Suet or lard   Birdseed
Grated cheese   Raisins

1. Ask an adult to make a small hole in the bottom of a yogurt pot. Thread string through the hole and tie a knot on the inside (make it long enough to tie to a tree).

2. Bring the suet/lard to room-temperature then cut into small pieces.

3. Add the suet/lard plus all other ingredients to the bowl and squidge it all together with your hands.

4. Fill your yogurt pots with the mixture and put them in the fridge for an hour or so to set.

5. Hang on a tree or bird table and become a birdwatcher!

Bird sounds

Birds often live in pairs or groups – they make sounds to attract mates, mark territory or to warn other birds of danger. Some songbirds are dull in colour, which **camouflages** them when nesting. You can't always see them, but you can certainly hear them!

Blackbirds

Often the first one up in the morning, singing sweet melodies.

FIELD ACTIVITY

Can you recreate some of the birds' songs with an instrument? Recorders are great for this.

Owls

Owls can make a **"t-wit twooo"** or **"hoohoo"** sound.

Ravens

Can you hear the **"kraa... kraa... kraa..."** of a raven?

Woodpeckers

Birds don't just call and sing, woodpeckers **"tap, tap, tap"** into tree trunks to find insect food, make nests and communicate with other woodpeckers.

BIRDS

Bats

Bats are the only **mammals** that can fly. They have thin, hollow bones, which make them light. Their delicate arm and finger bones form a frame, over which a thin layer of skin stretches to make wings.

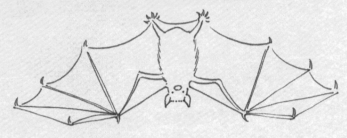

Hanging around

Bats are most active at night when they snatch up insects and other small animals. During the day they rest by hanging upside down on trees, under bridges or sometimes in caves.

Hearing their way

Most bats find their way in the dark using a process called **echolocation**, sending out high-pitched clicks through their mouth or nose. When the sounds hit an object, the echoes let the bat know how far away that object is.

FIELD FACT

The poo of a cave-dwelling bat is called guano – it is an excellent fertiliser for plants and people even pay for it!

Mighty mammals

A **mammal** is a warm-blooded **vertebrate** animal, often covered in hair or fur. Rodents are the largest group of **mammals** and are known for having sharp front teeth. Some mammals such as bats are **nocturnal** (active at night), whilst others like deer are **diurnal** (active in the day).

IMPORTANT NOTE

Wild animals can be dangerous. Never approach them and always watch from afar.

On the lookout

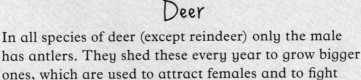

When you're out and about, you might catch a glimpse of an animal or hear something rustling. What might it be?

Deer

In all species of deer (except reindeer) only the male has antlers. They shed these every year to grow bigger ones, which are used to attract females and to fight rival males.

Fox

Foxes can live in towns or the countryside, but they are most active during the night. A fox's home is called a den.

Rabbit

Rabbits are one of the most commonly spotted **mammals**. They have large families, and they live in a system of **burrows** called a warren.

Wild boar

The wild boar belongs to the pig family. Like most pigs, it has excellent hearing and an even better sense of smell, helping it to find food buried in the ground.

Hedgehog

Hedgehogs are **nocturnal** animals that sleep all day. They love eating worms and slugs.

MAMMALS

Start searching!

With all of the nature facts you've read, you should be set for a bear hunt of your own. Bears can be found in the forests, grasslands and mountains across Europe, Asia, North America and South America. They are even found in the Arctic!

Bears

Bears are **mammals**. They are big and strong and tend to spend a lot of their time alone. Most bears are **omnivorous** (they eat both meat and plants).

FIELD FACT

Most bears will eat almost anything, including berries, roots, insects, salmon, deer and small **mammals**.

There are many types of bear in the world. Here are some of the most commonly known ones:

Black Bear

The black bear is not just black. It can have a lighter brown fur – and in some rare cases it can be white. It lives in forest and mountain **habitats** and has tall ears and short, black claws.

Grizzly Bear

The grizzly bear is larger and rarer than the black bear. It is intelligent and highly unpredictable. The grizzly bear can weigh up to an impressive 400 kilograms.

Polar Bear

Polar bears spend most of their time on sea ice, hunting seals. Their white fur means that they blend very well with the snowy backgrounds of their **habitats**.

Panda

Pandas are easily recognizable for the large, distinctive black patches around their eyes and body. Pandas love to eat bamboo.

FIELD ACTIVITY

During the ice age there was a cave bear that lived in Europe. Can you find out more about it?

The life of a bear

Bears that live in cooler places become less active in winter. They sleep in dens to avoid the cold and to save their energy. Bears can go for more than one hundred days without eating or drinking. Bears have an amazing sense of smell, and rely on this to find food.

IMPORTANT NOTE

If you spot a bear in real life, back away slowly. Walk, don't run, and make yourself look as big as possible.

Standing tall

Sometimes bears rear up onto their hind legs. They might do this if they're scared (to make themselves look bigger) or just to get a better view!

Bake your own bear paws

What better thing to do after a long day of nature watching than baking some yummy bear paw biscuits?

Ingredients:

250g butter (at room temp)
140g caster sugar
1 egg yolk
1 teaspoon vanilla extract
250g plain flour
50g cocoa powder
Chocolate buttons or whole blanched almonds

* Always ask for adult supervision and follow the recipe carefully.

1. Ask your adult to preheat the oven to 180°C /gas mark 4.

2. Beat the butter and sugar in a big bowl with a wooden spoon until it is light and fluffy.

3. Ask your adult to separate the egg. Add the yolk and the vanilla extract to your mixture. Stir until it is all combined.

4. Sift in the flour and cocoa powder and mix it all together until you have a nice thick dough.

5. Using your hands, shape the dough into thirty equal-sized balls and squash them down onto a baking tray.

6. Add chocolate buttons or almonds for the bears' claws.

7. Bake for 12–15 minutes. When they're ready, get your adult to transfer the biscuits onto a wire rack to cool.

BEARS

Keeping on Track

Paws for thought

To get one step closer to wildlife, it helps if you can identify paw prints, or tracks. Snow, mud and sand are excellent places to follow marks left by animals. Visit the woods, a riverbed or seashore and scan the ground carefully for evidence of prints.

IMPORTANT NOTE

Be careful when following tracks.
Never travel far by yourself – always
explore with an adult.

Take a look at which animals these prints belong to:

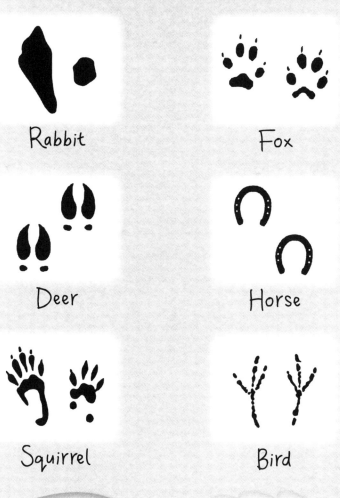

Rabbit

Fox

Deer

Horse

Squirrel

Bird

FIELD ACTIVITY

Have you spotted any animal prints? Can you identify them?

FIELD FACT

Some animals leave tail tracks too, like beavers.

A poo hunt!

Don't worry if you can't find any animal tracks – there are plenty of other signs that say there might be animal activity in your area.

Whose poo?

One of the things you can look for is animal poo (or "scat"). Animals don't just poo to get rid of waste – they do it as a way of sending messages to each other or marking territory.

IMPORTANT NOTE

Look, don't touch!
Animal poo can carry horrible germs.

Rabbit and hare poo

Rabbits and hares poo out round pellets, which contain finely chewed fragments of grass.

Fox poo

Fox poo looks like small dog droppings, and is often twisted at one end. Fresh ones smell very strong!

Squirrel poo

These cylindrical, 5mm-long pellets are deposited at random but can appear in large numbers beside a squirrel's favourite feeding spot.

Deer poo

Deer pellets are usually black and shiny when fresh. They can appear as one big clump and are often left in small piles in woods. The pellet size depends on the species.

Otter poo

Otter poo is called "spraint". It usually contains fish bones and is known for its strong smell! Otters leave their poo where it can be seen, such as on a rock or tree stump, so that another otter can tell if the poo's owner is male or female.

Look even closer

If you look closely, you may find other signs of animals living nearby. Fur, nests and chew marks are all things that indicate animal activity. Here are a few other pointers to look out for:

- Can you see signs of a **burrow**? Tread quietly and look for entrance holes – they are often among tree roots.

FIELD FACT

A good place to start is where animals feed, drink, bathe or gather.

Examine plants and trees carefully. Are they flattened or has anything been chewing, scratching or rubbing on them?

You may find an animal skeleton – either a creature that has died naturally or an animal that has been eaten by another animal. If you're lucky you might find an antler shed by a deer.

It's not always about what you can see. Can you hear any rustling or squawks? What can you smell?

The Big, Wide World

Threats to our world

The world is beautiful and hopefully after reading this book, you will have a better understanding of just how special it is. Such a wonderful place deserves to be looked after, but human activity is threatening our world.

Climate change

The climate of the earth has been changing. However the **climate change** people talk about today is to do with the impact of **global warming** – a gradual heating of the earth, which causes the type of weather we experience to change. For instance, as the earth heats up, glaciers melt and sea levels rise.

Pollution

There are a lot of people competing for the planet's resources, and we rely too much on **fossil fuels** (coal, oil and gas) which release deadly amounts of **carbon dioxide** into the **atmosphere**. But humans can't take all the blame – cows produce a massive amount of **methane** gas, which also adds to the **greenhouse effect**.

> **FIELD FACT**
>
> *Experts say that each cow can produce 250–500 litres of **methane** a day!*

What is global warming?

- The **greenhouse effect** is when the **atmosphere** that surrounds our planet traps some of the heat from the sun and keeps the earth warm.

- Without the **greenhouse effect**, the earth would be too cold for life to exist.

- However, as we burn **fossil fuels** more gases are released into the **atmosphere**. The more gases there are, the more heat becomes trapped by the **greenhouse effect**.

- This warming of the earth's surface and **atmosphere** is called **global warming**.

Sun

Atmosphere

Heat from the sun

Earth

The effects of global warming

Disappearing habitats

The North **Pole** and the South **Pole** may become
too warm for many of the creatures that live there.
Warming oceans are destroying parts of the coral reef.

Endangered species

Global warming will make life difficult for plants and
creatures all over the world. For example, if all the sea
ice disappears in the Arctic, polar bears may no longer
be able to survive.

Drought and flooding

Rising temperatures cause severe droughts,
which in turn causes crops to fail. Rising
sea levels mean that some islands may be
completely underwater in the next few years.

How can you help?

It's not too late to start saving our planet. There are a lot of little things you can do to be a bit friendlier to the world.

 Top tips to stay green

* Save electricity by wearing a jumper instead of turning the heating up.

* Save water by turning off the tap while you brush your teeth.

* **Reduce, reuse, recycle.** For instance: Reduce the amount of paper you use, or reuse old pieces of paper and recycle it when you are done with it!

* Plant bee-friendly flowers in your garden to create new **habitats**.

* Adopt or sponsor an endangered animal.

* Don't be a litterbug, as this can harm local wildlife.

FIELD FACT

Just as you leave footprints in mud, you also leave a carbon footprint behind. This is the amount of **carbon dioxide** *produced every time you use energy that comes from* **fossil fuels**.

Life is one big adventure and you
and your friends are the future.

If you can all do just some of these little things
for the planet, then you will help to keep
it beautiful for generations to come.

– *Glossary* –

Algae: a simple, non-flowering plant.

Amphibian: an animal that lives on the land and in the water.

Annelids: worms with ringed or segmented bodies.

Arthropod: a group of creatures that have jointed legs and hard outer skeletons.

Atmosphere: gases that surround our planet.

Bacteria: tiny organisms that can be harmful.

Blossoms: pretty flowers that cover fruit trees in the spring.

Burrow: a hole or tunnel dug by a small animal for shelter.

Calcite: a mineral found in limestone.

Camouflage: colouring or patterns that allow an animal to blend in with its surroundings.

Carbon dioxide: the gas formed when carbon is burned, or when people and animals breathe out.

Chrysalis: the stage at which a caterpillar turns into an adult butterfly or moth.

Climate change: changes in the weather patterns around the world.

Condensation: water vapour, which changes back to a liquid.

Constellation: a group of stars that form a pattern in the night sky.

Crystals: hard substances formed when minerals heat up or cool down.

Deciduous: plants that lose their leaves in autumn.

Dissolve: when a solid mixes with a liquid to form a solution.

Diurnal: animals that are active during the day.

Echolocation: a process where animals use sound to "see" their way in the dark.

Environment: the conditions that surround a living creature.

Erosion: the wearing away of rock or soil by forces such as water or wind.

Evaporation: when water turns into vapour.

Evergreen: trees that look green all year round.

Fossil fuels: natural fuels that release carbon dioxide.

Fungi: organisms such as mushrooms that feed on organic material.

Global warming: a gradual increase in the temperature of the earth's atmosphere.

Glucose: an important source of energy for animals and plants.

Gravity: a force that tries to pull two objects towards each other.

Greenhouse effect: when the atmosphere surrounding earth traps heat from the sun.

Habitat: the natural home of an animal, plant or organism.

Lichen: a simple slow-growing plant.

Mammal: a warm-blooded vertebrate.

Margin: a word that describes the edges of a leaf.

Metamorphosis: the several different stages of life before becoming an adult.

Methane: a colourless, odourless gas.

Migrate: move from one habitat to another according to the seasons.

Mollusc: animals with soft, unsegmented bodies.

Mouth: where a river enters a lake, larger river or the sea.

Nocturnal: animals that are active at night.